DEMOS

Demos is an independent think tank committed to radical thinking on the long-term problems facing the UK and other advanced industrial societies.

It aims to develop ideas – both theoretical and practical – to help shape the politics of the twenty first century, and to improve the breadth and depth of political debate.

Demos publishes books and a quarterly journal and undertakes substantial empirical and policy oriented research projects. Demos is a registered charity.

In all of its work Demos brings together people from a wide range of backgrounds in business, academia, government, the voluntary sector and the media to share and cross-fertilise ideas and experiences.

For further information and
subscription details please write to:
Demos, 9 Bridewell Place, London EC4V 6AP
Tel 0171 353 4479 Fax 0171 353 4481
email: mail@demos.co.uk

Escaping poverty
From safety nets to networks of opportunity

Perri 6

First published in
September 1997

by

Demos
9 Bridewell Place
London EC4V 6AP
Tel: 0171 353 4479
Fax: 0171 353 4481

Arguments 13

ISBN 1 898309 88 4

CONTENTS

Introduction

To tackle the continuing miseries of poverty and long-term unemployment, frailty in old age and alienation and suicide among young people in Britain, we need to enable people to develop and sustain the right kind of social network to thrive for their stage of life.

For too long, we have ignored the importance of social networks in the design of welfare policies because we have assumed that some combination of incentives and skills are sufficient to tackle the problems of social exclusion.

Having access to, and the ability to make use of, the right kind of social network is often necessary to be able to thrive. Of course, other things are necessary to help people to get themselves out of a variety of conditions of misery. Having the right kind of network will not of itself create jobs or produce new cures for diseases or rebuild dilapidated housing estates. But even if our economy creates new jobs, if medical research generates new cures and if money is found to rehabilitate our worst rented housing, poverty and illness will destroy many more lives than they need to, if our policies continue to stimulate the wrong kinds of social networks.

Moreover, networks are not just something individuals can make and use for themselves. They are relationships with many others. But people cannot use them if they do not exist. In some of the most deprived places, the fabric of social networks has become so derelict that individual solutions will not be enough to enable people to make their exit from poverty.

Throughout the western world in the 1990s, there has been a growing belief that the apparently intractable problems of poverty are something to do with social exclusion and with a lack of social capital – both terms that have lacked a clear definition. In Part I of this *Argument*, I try to give a clear meaning to social exclusion and lack of social capital as 'network poverty'. Using evidence from recent research, I show that this kind of poverty is one of a number of risk factors which harm people's ability to thrive at any given stage of the life course.

Part II addresses the policy implications of this analysis. It reviews the effects of many of our welfare state policies on social networks among poor and disadvantaged people at different stages in the life course and argues that they are perverse. Finally, it sets out some recommendations on how reform might proceed.

The argument is that there is no point in debating how to finance the future of welfare, unless we create a system of support for the poor and socially excluded which enables them to develop the kinds of social network they need.

Part 1. Understanding network poverty

'Network poverty' is a real and important problem for many people and it takes different forms at different stages of the life course. I begin by reviewing evidence about the kinds of network poverty that prevent adults from thriving in the labour market, and then turn to the kinds that prevent children, adults and frail elderly people from thriving in learning, health and longevity. Finally, I use this evidence to define the concept of network poverty and show how it relates to social capital.

It's not just who you know, but how you know them 1: weak ties

The evidence
Recent research gives us a good picture of the configurations of social networks that seem to characterise adults who do well in the labour market and in the world of organisations – in getting jobs, in getting contracts or business or promotion, in sustaining higher levels of complex organisations, or just in securing a middle class lifestyle.

Middle class and working class lives
It is a reasonably well-established finding in the sociology of class, to quote a recent study of Britain in the post-war decades, that

> The patterns of informal sociability of the working class are more likely than those of the middle class to revolve around close contacts with kin and a small set of friends, all of whom are relatively closely connected with each other. On the whole, these are likely to be friends of long standing, often old school friends. By contrast, the social networks of the middle class tend to be much more extensive and diverse. They are likely to see twice as many colleagues from work fairly regularly outside the workplace; they draw their friends from a more diverse range of sources and those friends are often not closely connected to each other. Perhaps surprisingly, those in the

middle class are also likely to know twice as many of their neighbours fairly well than do those in the working class; and much smaller numbers suffer from a complete absence of social support. Finally those in the middle class seem less likely to limit their interaction with friends to a particular sphere or activity in favour of engaging them in multiple kinds of endeavours.[1]

For the middle classes, who have always been the principal consumers of higher education, college and university are key sites for the making of contacts who will become useful in later life. In the 1990s, as working hours have lengthened and job insecurity has become more deeply felt, middle class people may be becoming more instrumental and calculating in consciously working their networks as a strategy for coping with labour market pressures: certainly, some commentators have detected more of an instrumental tenor to the weak tie friendships of middle class people.[2]

The class distinction in types of networks may now be breaking down in some parts of the country. One study has shown that even in working class areas, friends are more important than relatives or neighbours in helping with shopping, cleaning, keeping an eye on the house and the like.[3] Gradually, for all classes, the roles of friends and kin may converge, at least during adult life.[4] Moreover, those low skilled and low income working class people who are not in mainstream jobs in manufacturing, extraction or services but are in marginal employment or in the informal economy, have long made most use of networks of strangers and casual contacts to make a living.[5] But, as we shall see, sharp differences remain between the social networks available to people, at least at the extremes of wealth and poverty.

Getting a job

A quarter of a century ago, in a now very well-known paper, 'The strength of weak ties', American sociologist Mark Granovetter demonstrated not only that people get jobs through working their contacts, but that the most valuable contacts are not the ones with whom they have strong ties, such as kin and neighbours, but those with whom they have weak ties, such as former colleagues, acquaintances and friends of friends.[6] Weak ties lead people less frequently to direct offers of jobs than to information, to opportunities and, in some situations, to patronage. The process by which weak tie networks are used changes them, making them more dense, complex and further reaching over time.[7]

Granovetter defined the strength of a tie between individuals as 'a (probably linear) combination of the amount of time, the emotional intensity, the intimacy (mutual confiding) and the reciprocal services which characterise the tie'.[8] In short, the extent of trust is key. In practice, most people have their strongest ties with kin and some people may have close ties with immediate neighbours. But weak ties prove to be more useful in advancing oneself in the labour market.

Many studies have confirmed this finding.[9] In particular, a well-known British study of a DHSS cohort of unemployed people in the 1980s strikingly bore out Granovetter's findings. More of that cohort found employment through friends and personal contacts than through any other single route.[10] The Labour Force Survey show a growing reliance on informal methods of job search, although not necessarily at the expense of formal methods, while the General Household Survey reports that these informal network strategies are typically more successful.[11] The same phenomenon has been found recently in a study of welfare recipients in Philadelphia.[12] In the United States, a very large panel study of the illegal immigrants whose status was regularised following the 1986 amnesty found that personal contact using acquaintances at least as often as kin was the principal means of job search and the most successful in securing a first job; the same finding was reproduced for subsequent jobs and promotions.[13]

Getting on in business

More recently, a Chicago-based sociologist of business, Ronald Burt, has shown that the same configuration of social networks explains how the more effective business firms and individual managers within them perform so well. Individuals who do well have networks which span what he calls 'structural holes', or major gaps, in the fabric of contacts and links that makes up the world of business. They have links to people who are unlike themselves, they ensure that their links span a wide diversity of holes, and they maintain only one or a few

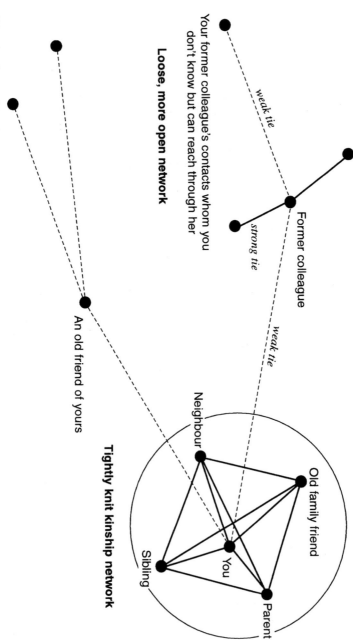

Figure 1. weak ties can span holes in the social structure and reach parts other ties cannot reach

Friends of your friend

Your former colleague's contacts whom you
don't know but can reach through her

Loose, more open network

weak tie

Former colleague

strong tie

weak tie

An old friend of yours

Neighbour

Old family friend

Tightly knit kinship network

Sibling

You

Parent

key links to each cluster, minimising 'redundancy' in their networks.[14] These individuals are brokers, matchers of individuals with news and gossip, movers of opportunities to people who can use them. What works at the individual level works well at the social level in business: a network that is rich in such people will do better, on average, than one that does not attract them or cultivate such skills among its existing members.

Figure 1 shows in simple graphical terms a network configuration with weak ties that span 'structural holes' between clusters and contrasts a dense network with a lot of redundancy – many routes to each individual – and one with little redundancy.

According to Burt, any individual's social capital can properly be understood as the set of access routes to other key individuals who can offer information or other resources necessary for that individual to perform well.[15]

Unemployment

Many studies of long-term benefit claimants have found evidence of social isolation. For example a well-known, small scale study in the early 1990s found very low levels of social engagement by claimants outside their immediate family.[16] Importantly, rather few were resigned to this experience, although a very few positively adopted the cultural role of 'proud outcast' in response (see the appendix for more on this). The survey of the DHSS cohort found that lack of company was one of the most widely felt costs of being jobless.[17]

A recent French study also found that long-term unemployed individuals had weaker family and social ties than other groups, although the author regarded this principally as a consequence of unemployment. However, the study argued that weak social networks in general were characteristic of those people on the margins of the labour market and defined a concept of 'relational poverty', measured by the self-reported quality of family, friendship and community relationships. The long-term unemployed and marginally employed had the highest scores of relational poverty in this aggregated sense.[18]

A recent study compared long-term and short-term unemployed people with people in work in six towns across England and Scotland, using a composite measure of sociability combining participation in sporting, leisure and social activities weighted both by the number of other people involved and by the frequency of participation. It found that unemployed people fared much worse and, among them, single people fared still worse than other unemployed people. Their sample of unemployed people divided evenly between those who saw friends less after becoming unemployed and those who did not. Over half had friendship networks, of which more than half were also unemployed. Most of those unemployed people whose friendship networks included significant numbers of people in employment also reported that they had stronger support systems.[19] Fewer than one third of the unemployed members of their sample could think of someone they knew who could help them to get a job, whereas over two fifths of the employed and self-employed could think of such a person in their networks.[20] The authors commented that unemployment may well not have caused this impoverishment of social networks; rather, it is possible that 'other unmeasured background variables' were at work.[21] On the other hand, they note that 'the segregation of the unemployed into social networks that consisted largely of other unemployed people thus increased their vulnerability in the face of psychological and financial hardship and was likely to have made it more difficult to escape from unemployment itself'.[22]

Data have been analysed from the 1991 wave of the British Household Panel Survey comparing the proportions of employed and unemployed respondents claiming that no one was available to listen to them, to help in a crisis, to relax with, to really appreciate the respondent or to offer comfort. On each of these measures with the exception of the first ('listen'), significantly more of the unemployed made these claims.[23]

This picture is confirmed by a 1989 study of unemployed people in Hartlepool.[24] Most unemployed people had partners and close male kin who were also unemployed and the majority of their friends were also unemployed, creating a partial social segregation between the employed and unemployed.[25] Informal methods of job search including the working of networks of kin and acquaintance were the most likely to be successful. The insecurely employed were most reliant on informal networks.

In the Hartlepool study, most people had networks dominated principally by strong ties to kin and neighbours and people like themselves. The author suggests that, in conditions of high unemployment, a sense of greater obligation to kin may reassert itself in the selection of people to whom information about jobs is passed.[26]

While this is entirely understandable and rational *in the short term*, it is not clear that it constitutes the best strategy if it keeps individuals within areas of long-term economic decline. *In the long term*, a superior strategy for those individuals might well be to make greater use of weak ties outside the community to secure jobs elsewhere. Of course, mass exit does not typically produce the best outcome for those left behind, as has been shown by the experience of Liverpool's depopulation, but there may well be ways in which intelligent social policy can enable people to make better use of their weak ties while economic regeneration policies give them reasons to use them within their locality.

Poor and disadvantaged areas

In the US, William Julius Wilson has contended that ghettos are socially isolated from the rest of the network fabric that makes up America.[27] He emphasises the importance of contact with thriving individuals who can act as role models to enable exit from poverty. He also stresses the importance of concentration effects – that the experience of being poor in an area where everyone you meet and know is also poor is much worse and more damaging for long-term prospects of exit from poverty than being poor in a more affluent area.

The ghetto is a social enclave. Few people have friends outside it or friends unlike themselves.[28] In particular, he argues, having a social network in which most kin, friends and neighbours are unemployed, in marginal or unstable employment or poor reinforces doubts about one's ability to make an exit. This can, over time, reinforce discouragement and a culture of fatalism.[29] These 'ecological' or 'spatial' effects are readily understood in terms of social networks that are bounded both geographically and socially by class and race.[30] As the relatively few African-Americans able to achieve upward social mobility move out of the ghettos, they are lost as role models to those left behind. In such a context, social networks cannot perform the function of securing access to labour market opportunities that they can in areas where many people have weak ties.[31] In the ghetto, then, people have to rely mainly on formal labour market institutions and may not be able effectively to create and sustain new organisations. In the worst ghettos, it can be argued, the problem is that social networks have atrophied to the point that they cannot be used effectively even if people had the skills and willingness to use them.

Sustaining organisation
Still more recently, a major study of how social capital makes societies sustain higher levels of organisation, and hence of competitiveness, concluded that a key indicator is the extent to which individuals are able to trust those who are not kin and immediate neighbours with responsibility as their agents. Societies in which people are willing to trust those who are not kin to take on senior positions in their family firms produce much more complex and larger organisations which can survive the succession problems that dog small family firms. Such societies, the author argues, often prove economically more competitive than those in which trust remains within families and immediate neighbours.[32]

Adults need weak ties to brokers
From these studies, a single message emerges relentlessly. As an adult in the labour force, having a network that is rich in weak ties which span holes in social networks to reach acquaintances and friends of friends across many walks of life proves to be much more effective – at least in the long run – than having a narrow network of strong ties to kin, immediate neighbours and people much like oneself.

Of course, strong ties continue to matter in adult life, even for thriving in the labour market. In order to reach one's first weak ties, an individual may start with their strong ties. A young person entering the labour market will often use their parents' or close relatives' contacts. There are also weak ties that seem to work by mimicking strong ties.[33] For example, appealing to a potential employer or an individual who can offer information about work opportunities on the basis of some shared identity, such as having been to the same school or university or attending the same church, can sometimes be an effective strategy: shared identity can a basis for initial willingness to trust.[34] While such initial sources of contact may be of continuing importance in areas of economic decline, where competition for jobs is high and as traditional loyalties reassert themselves, in more favourable circumstances weak ties may gradually prove more useful over the life course, even for working class people wanting to remain in their declining locality.[35]

The most valuable ties are with people who can offer access to other networks. They are, in effect, *brokers*. For example, a worker who brings someone who is a friend of a friend or a former colleague into a job at their own firm will gain credit both with the new employee and with the company (assuming the new recruit is a success). These individuals are network entrepreneurs and identifying them, or persuading individuals to act as such, is a particularly valuable skill for adults to acquire in their labour market strategies.[36] However, it is not necessary for thriving that people consciously and calculatingly exploit their friends and acquaintances. Too obvious an instrumental style in 'networking' can even be counter-productive.

Work provides an important institution for social mixing, where people can make new weak ties and find potential brokers. But there are other institutions which perform this role. In some communities, churches, schools, charities and state agencies that provide opportunities for mixing while volunteering together (and even Usenet groups operating across the Internet) can be important sites for making and sustaining weak ties.

Cause or effect?

One might think that having a network configuration which is lacking in hole-spanning weak ties is a consequence of one's situation but is not particularly significant as a cause of being in poverty. Not being in work, one doesn't have colleagues, doesn't get invited to conferences and training events or even to the pub after work. Without the income from a wage, one can't afford the travel costs of maintaining links with geographically distant people and can't sustain the expenditure on social dining, lunching and 'networking' at parties or receptions that people in work can and do. Not being in the thick of things, one has less information of value to offer to other people who, in the ordinary run of reciprocity, have less reason to offer you information of value.

Of course, young unemployed people who have not yet had a job will not have been able to build up complex and diverse networks of contacts, colleagues and former colleagues and those from working class backgrounds may well not have inherited them from parents, family friends or school and college contacts. This group is the least likely to get jobs on the strength of their own contacts and more likely to rely on formal means of job search and application.

The evidence from the studies of American ghettos and the formation of large businesses, and the cross-sectional correlation data on long-term, unemployed people, may not be conclusive about the direction of causality between networks with insufficient numbers of weak ties and failing to thrive economically. Nevertheless, it does appear likely that at least in some cases inadequate social networks may be a prior characteristic of people's lives.[37]

Certainly, having networks that are poor in weak ties is an effect, for many people, of unemployment and poverty. But not for all. Many of the studies cited above showed that at least some unemployed and poor people do sustain networks that span structural holes and at least some people make their exit from unemployment and poverty and even into the middle class. It is quite possible that these individuals or households exhibit a quite different network configuration from those who fail to make their exit.

One major study found that entrants into the middle class had roughly the same number of organisational links and friends as people born into the middle class. Importantly, they drew less on kin and *more* on contacts made through voluntary associations even than those who were born into and remain in the middle class, and certainly more than those who remained in the working class.[38] The fact that, for example, *fully one half* of the sample of unemployed people in the study in six English and Scottish towns mentioned above did *not* seem greatly isolated suggests not only diversity of networks among the poor, but the possibility that those with richer networks may be the ones better able, all other things being equal, to make their exit.[39] Certainly, we need to know much more about these 'invulnerables' and those who successfully achieve upward mobility.

Interactions of network poverty and other risk factors

It is important to distinguish between risk factors for two distinct life events – entry into unemployment and failing to exit from it.[40] While it is unlikely that 'network poverty' is, of itself, sufficient to make an individual long-term unemployed, it is at the very least an important risk factor for failing to find one's way out of long-term unemployment. A brief review of the main literature on unemployment suggests that there is a broad consensus on what the main risk factors are for each of these events.[41]

Of course, some factors may be important in explaining both events, while others may be more important for just one. For example, factors concerned with the demand for labour – recessions, for example – may be much more important in explaining the likelihood of entry into unemployment at any one time, but lacking hole-spanning weak ties partly explains the failure of at least some groups of unemployed people to exit from unemployment after one or two years.

A simple, and rather aggregated, classification of the main risk factors for entry into and failure to exit from unemployment might look like Figure 2 (see page 20). I have chosen what seem to be the most causally important factors and stripped out most of the demographic characteristics – with the exception of age – that appear only to be significant because they are strongly associated with one or more of these causally significant features.

The interactions between these factors will be complex. Focusing just on the supply side forces listed in Figure 2, one way to think about these interactions is as follows. Three forces – family background, age and previous unemployment – are wholly independent variables, unaffected by others. By contrast, most of the others will presumably interact with one another. The cultural and social network structure variables – mobility, skills, reserve wage, performance – are likely to have the most complex interactions with each other. A far as I am aware, there has not yet been any empirical study in Britain that has sought to test a model which elaborates on these interactions or identifies the relative strength of the causal interactions. However, some of the individual links are reasonably well established from other research.

The interaction between social networks and culture is particularly important in explaining why some people fail to make their exit from long-term unemployment and poverty. Much of the debate about welfare reform over the past twenty years has focused on how to change 'cultures of dependency' and whether they are a sensible way to understand the reasons why people do not make their own way out.

Figure 2. Risk factors for entry into and failure to exit from unemployment

Entry		Failure to exit		
Demand side	**Supply side**		**Demand side**	**Supply side**
Low demand in industry of last job Low demand in region of residence Changing demand by skill, experience, discrimination patterns	(P) Performance: poor performance in work, attitude, reliability, loyalty (I) Immobility: unwillingness or inability to relocate or retrain (S) Skill: lack of skills, experience or educational achievement (PU) Previous unemployment (F) Family and home background	*Willingness to exit*		(C) Culture: discouragement, low aspiration, culture of fatalism, dependency or 'drop-out' culture (R) Reserve wage greater than wage on offer because (a) benefit trap (b) prestige, status (c) costs of working eg travel, childcare (d) other costs eg debt, drugs
		Ability to exit	'Insider' effects in industrial relations, information, opportunities Employer discrimination in recruitment against long-term unemployed or older workers	(N) Social network structure (A) Age (S) Skills: lack of skills, experience or educational achievement

A clear understanding of the role of social networks in influencing the cultures – and they are plural – will suggest a more useful starting point for debating welfare reform. Cultures do matter and changing them is important, but not in the ways that some of those who talk about cultures of dependency think. The appendix sets out in more detail one way of thinking about the links between social networks and cultures among long-term unemployed people.

In Part II, I argue that while we may have in place many policy instruments for tackling poverty, some of these measures have perverse effects upon the social network structures of poor and unemployed people.

Criminal networks, exclusive clubs and destructive social capital

There are plenty of kinds of network, where the structure or configuration will provide the means to thrive at least in the short term. But we must not celebrate *any* kind of exit from poverty, any kind of network or any kind of social capital. The consequences of a person participating in some networks may be very damaging for everyone else and perhaps, in the longer term, for themselves.

Socially beneficial and socially damaging networks cannot always readily be distinguished by the kinds of ties that dominate them, or the satisfaction with those ties that individuals feel. For example, young delinquents show no great differences from non-delinquent youths in the likelihood of being socially isolated, the structural characteristics of their family ties, friendships, peer groups and networks or their feelings about these links.[42]

Strong tie networks can easily be negative: child abuse happens within the closest families. Criminal networks can provide at least some people with a diverse set of weak ties, and the more organised and business-like the criminal network, the more it will resemble the networks of successful business. It may well be that at least some criminal organisations tend to begin with strong short ties, in conditions of isolation from and distrust of the wider society, with oaths perhaps mimicking the bonds that are normally found in strong ties of kinship, as has been argued in the case of the Sicilian Mafia.[43]

These cases of criminal, enclavist, strongly tied networks with a small number of weak hole-spanning ties seem to be small in number and quite distinctive.

Many networks can be exclusive, with damaging consequences for the wider society. Working men's clubs, white racist tenants' associations, closed 'old boy networks' in firms and organisations, are all examples of enclavist network structures that have established hierarchical and exclusive relationships with outsiders in the effort to preserve their social capital.

This also suggests that for marginalised communities, enclavist strategies that stress community autonomy, self-reliance and internal trading, and rejection of integration may not be optimal. While these strategies may have short-term appeal to community pride, particularly for ethnic groups victimised by racism, they may prove damaging in the longer term.[44]

In various ways, it is possible to thrive using network wealth that imposes costs on others. Nevertheless, it is clear from the various pieces of evidence reviewed in this *Argument*, that *for the most part* and *in the long run*, more open and extensive systems of contact and trust than are common in most of the criminal and socially discriminatory networks prove to be better strategies for adult individuals.

It's not just who you know, but how you know them 2: strong ties

So far, I have been concerned only with the network configurations necessary for adults to thrive in the labour market. In this section, I shall argue that the social network configurations necessary to thrive in respect of health for children, adults and frail elderly people, and to thrive in a number of other respects for adolescents, look very different. Indeed, for these groups, the social networks they need to thrive are quite the reverse of those for adults in the labour market, because they require strong ties.

Child health

It is obvious that children, first and foremost, need for their successful physical and psychological development strong ties to their parents and at most a small number of adults within the family. In that sense, the findings of the psychological theory of attachment are not in the least controversial. There is a large body of research on child health showing the clear link between children's psychological and physical health status and network configuration dominated by strong ties.[45] The current widespread concern, on both sides of the usual left/right debates, about the strength of family ties and the risks that children face when these are weakened reflects this. While community level action may be necessary in this field – such as more family-friendly work practices – the important network ties are the strong, short ones within the immediate circle of family and neighbours.

Youth homelessness

It is clear from the most recent research into the characteristics of the young, homeless people who are now so visible on the streets of the major British cities, that the largest single cause of their homelessness is breakdown of family relationships, leading to their being evicted or leaving home.[46] Many have been in local authority care and are without strong family ties.[47] While a few of the young homeless form rather enclavist and 'drop-out' networks with other street homeless people, leading some to talk of a culture of homelessness, most appear isolated. Lack of strong ties appears to be a principal cause of, or at least a risk factor attributing to, their entry into homelessness and their failure to exit from it. Indeed, the findings of one recent study which examined the aspirations of homeless people stressed the importance of rebuilding a lost family or the family never possessed[48] and their sense of their need for support.[49]

Adult health

While adults need weak ties to thrive in the labour market, adult mental and physical health depends on a reasonable balance of strong and weak ties.

Isolation and lack of social support in particular are risk factors for many conditions, including depression[50] and stress.[51] Indeed, many of the signs of fatalism, retreat and discouragement observed in discouraged, long-term, unemployed workers sound remarkably like the symptoms of depression. Poor quality of social support has been linked with cardiovascular disease through low production of the protein Apo-AI which helps to protect against atherosclerosis.[52] However, we do not know enough about the exact balance of strong and weak ties that makes better general health in the long term.

Frail elderly people
In the first decades of retirement, one of the most important factors in maintaining psychological and physical health is the sustaining of activity and associated social networks, often with weak ties linked to previous employment and other institutions in which people develop themselves. However, in extreme old age, when frailty and dependence begin to set in, the network configurations that make for health change significantly.

The most sophisticated study of the types of network that elderly people need to thrive has been done by gerontologist Claire Wenger. In a series of studies over the last decade, she has identified different kinds of support networks; these are summarised in Figure 3 in order from the most to the least supportive.[53] Although each of the network types presents its own risks, she finds that those elderly people who thrive best through their increasing frailty are those whose networks are locally integrated and wider community focused.

Wenger's finding demonstrates the central importance of strong, short ties, with a great deal of ties between the persons linked to the individual. This is quite the reverse of the networks dominated by weak, hole-spanning ties with low redundancy that Burt and Granovetter found to be crucial to adults in the labour market and much more similar to the configurations required by children for their psychological and physical well-being.

Figure 3. Wenger's taxonomy of support networks of elderly people

Type of support network	Typical circumstances
locally integrated	local relative carer, support from friends and neighbours, shared care
wider community focused	family makes short-term, helping visits but does not offer long-term, informal care, friends withdraw when dependency increases
local self-contained	little relative support, neighbours monitor, no informal care unless by spouse
local family dependent	long-term care by spouse or relative with other family support
private restricted	alone or isolated spouse carer, no other source of care

Source: Wenger, 1997.

Secondary weak ties remain important even in extreme old age. Some of the support available from carers, particularly from those who may themselves be becoming frail, may often come from people with whom they have weaker ties than they have with kin. And to some extent, it is possible to substitute weak ties for strong ties, by buying in care. However, because of the trust problems involved in having relative strangers perform the most intimate services, many elderly people prefer to avoid wholesale substitution if they can.

The network transitions

If, at the beginning and end of life, networks dominated by strong ties with at least some 'redundancy' are important and perhaps necessary to thrive but reversed during adult life, then managing the transition between these differing network configurations becomes crucial.

Many of the poor, the young unemployed who have never had a job, the long-term unemployed and, in the extreme case, the young homeless, as well as many of the frail elderly who are isolated or dependent on a few family members who cannot meet their needs, may well be people who have not been able, for one reason or another, to manage these 'network transitions' effectively.

During the transition into adult life, strong ties may well be a very important basis, but where, for example, they are too strong, maturation may not proceed. And where parents attempt to keep them exclusive, they may find the ties become brittle as adolescents increasingly need new networks of their own. Initially, adolescents may try to make their weak ties emulate strong ones – witness the 'best friend' syndrome and the oaths of loyalty that bind gangs into strong enclaves. However, as maturation progresses they learn to accept weak ties for what they are.[54]

Dealing with individuals with whom one has or would like to have weak ties involves developing certain skills of etiquette, vocabulary and communication. Children whose parents use their weak ties – perhaps more often in the middle class – will observe these skills in use and may be able readily to emulate them. One has to learn codes for dressing, responding to social cues, conversing, requesting and giving across classes, disciplines and geographical boundaries. By contrast, those who observe their parents using only the skills for strong ties may find these skills harder to learn.[55]

In the first few months or even years of job search, young people may have to borrow their parents' or other near kin's weak ties in order to secure jobs through informal contact. Quite quickly, they will learn to make their own weak tie contacts and make use of them.

The transition into frailty in old age can be similarly difficult to manage, as adults find it hard to accept a loss of independence. Older people's networks tend to be dominated by peers of the same age and more subject to loss by death than younger adults' networks. However, with the onset of ill-health and particularly confusions, dementias or incontinence, friends and sometimes neighbours tend to withdraw. Being thus thrown back on strong ties can be a hurtful experience, which makes the transition more difficult to bear. Those people with very tightly knit family-centred networks are often less successful in thriving, because their networks are less likely to alert the sources of professional support.

Transitions are not simply processes by which needs to thrive call for one network configuration rather than another. Because networks are so central to our identity and roles in life, they are also periods when people make changes in their culture, reflected in changing perceptions of risk, world views, stances toward what they perceive as the mainstream of social order. Because changing one's network involves changing one's culture, it is often difficult to make these transitions.

Network poverty, social exclusion, social capital, trust and culture

Network poverty can be defined as follows:

> The network poor are individuals who do not have the kind of social network configuration that is most appropriate for the stage of the life course they have reached, to enable them to thrive – where thriving can be a matter of securing good health, securing emotional support and development or maturity, securing work and income and status and a high level of consumption, or simply prolonging a life in reasonable comfort.

Within the general category of the network poor, we can distinguish the following four types of network poverty.

- *isolation*, or lacking both sufficient weak, hole-spanning and sufficient strong, short ties
- *weak tie poverty:* in adult life, a network dominated by strong ties that do not span holes to diverse walks of life, where those with whom one has ties are densely linked to each other creating redundancy in one's network, or where few of those with whom one has weak ties can act as network brokers
- *strong tie poverty:* in childhood or extreme old age, a network dominated by weak ties but lacking in strong ties to kin and immediate neighbours, and where the people with whom one has ties are not sufficiently linked to one another to ensure cooperation in one's support
- *network transition poverty:* at the points of transition during adolescence or in the early years in the labour market, and from active 'third age' retirement to frailty or 'fourth age' dependency in extreme old age, inability or unwillingness to make the transition

from one kind of network configuration to another better suited to one's changing needs.

In general, we can say that, all other things being equal, any kind of network poverty will be a major risk factor for, and in some cases perhaps even the principal cause of, poverty, unemployment, homelessness, ill-health and other forms of misery.

There has been a debate for some time about how to measure poverty multi-dimensionally, because simple 'poverty lines' measured in wealth or income are obviously inadequate to capture all that deprivation means. Some of the multi-dimensional measures of poverty include, as one dimension, weakness in or damage to 'family ties', 'social support', 'community', 'participation', 'social relations' or 'social networks'.[56] The problem with most of these measures is that they fail to distinguish between the role of strong and weak ties, between the network needs of different stages of the life course and between different causal effects of different kinds of network poverty. They have sometimes tended to suggest that the crucial issue is either the crude number of ties possessed or the affective commitment and depth of support offered, rather than the network configuration, which explains the role and value of numbers or 'quality' of ties. The definition offered above therefore represents an advance in the sophistication both of measurement requirements and of understanding of how the dynamics of poverty work.

In fact, this definition and classification of network poverty amounts to a definition of *social exclusion*. 'Social exclusion' is a term used in various ways in French, American and other political discourse about poverty, where it connotes variously relative inequality, simple, long-term unemployment, very low social status or stigma or membership of 'the underclass', and so on.[57] By defining social exclusion in terms of one's place in the fabric of social networks, the term acquires a clear and useful meaning for policy makers.[58] But more importantly, it makes it clear that social exclusion is likely to be a cause of poverty in adulthood and of other kinds of failure to thrive in childhood and old age, as well as one of its effects.

By contrast, the absence of network poverty or network wealth is a key foundation stone in the definition of *social capital*.[59] The conventional sociological definition of social capital is that it consists in valued relationships with significant others[60] or participation in social relationships or networks in which trust, cooperation, reciprocity and norms can develop.[61] However, sociologists have begun to argue recently that social capital is often at its most valuable when it is found in ties that 'link substantial sectors of the community and span social cleavages'.[62]

Taking social networks seriously suggests a more coherent way of classifying and understanding social capital through the following tiers, which are ordered by increasing commitment, moral content and effort required to sustain them:

- *shared identity*: which can be recognised even by strangers without a conversation, for example by clothing, deportment, obvious ethnicity or religion[63]
- *network*: ties of varying strength to others involving some kind of social intercourse and at least a minimal level of trust – that each party regards the other's statements of intent as credible[64] and the tie worth persisting with; the wider the structural span of the tie, bridging holes and gaps in the social fabric between classes, cliques and clusters, the greater its private and public value
- *resources*: the practice of making resources such as information, introductions, opportunities or gossip available to people across network ties[65]
- *affectivity*: goodwill, fellowship, sympathy, trust that commitments will be honoured and one's interests taken into account, commitment to individuals with whom one has network ties[66]
- *norms*: acceptance of moral duties or obligations, rules, principles of conduct such as reciprocity, mutuality[67]
- *skills*: capacities to create structure, organisation and formal legal entities, entitlements, obligations, contracts.[68]

It is, however, misleading to confuse the organisations which are the products of social capital with social capital itself – particularly as they can sometimes destroy the social capital required to assemble them. In particular, the self-serving claim by voluntary organisations alone to *be* social capital or that their numbers and health are reliable signs of its existence should be resisted.[69]

This understanding suggests that the system of social networks provides a basis on which the more complex and demanding tiers of social capital can be built. The classification suggests that social capital may be *reflexive*: that is, as higher order tiers are built and sustained, they will normally reinforce the network foundations. Network poverty is, therefore, a failure in one of the key foundations of social capital.

What passes across the ties within networks, then, is some kind of trust and commitment. Weak ties, by definition, require less trust and commitment than strong ones. Weakly tied individuals offer others opportunities to trade, to gain access to information, help in finding work. They are typically concerned with occasional transactions and the expectation is that, sooner or later, the balance of benefit will be roughly equal between the parties. By contrast, strong ties are the ones where trust and commitment is greater. Goodwill trust – trust that one will go beyond the terms of any contract or legal duty in order to act in the other's interests – is required and some ties can achieve absolute trust, in which one no longer trusts the other person to do anything in particular, but one simply trusts them, *tout court*.[70]

Network poverty is centrally a deficit in the means of securing trust. It is therefore not surprising that it is strongly associated with a culture of fatalism, in which people have little trust either in the reliability of systems or of other persons. Isolation is but one form of network poverty, but in cultural terms it appears to be quite similar to the other kinds: it is associated, increasingly over the period of isolation, with enclavism or retreatism. Those who are able to make their exit from poverty, using social capital in the form of network wealth, tend to be those with other kinds of culture which enables trust (see appendix).

Networks are systems of communication and they are lumpy. Markets, governments and every kind of social organisation are embedded in them,[71] run on them[72] and in turn produce new forms of them. Global market society is increasingly organised around networks of information which move beyond traditional institutional and organisational boundaries but which are costly for individuals to enter.[73] 'Networking' is an accepted way to organise one's life and a sign of thriving. This is why social exclusion or network poverty is perhaps one of the most stigmatised dimension of poverty.

Part II. Combating network poverty

What is being done and what could be done to tackle network poverty? I will argue that much of what is done in the name of state welfare is in fact producing perverse effects. It discourages or even disables people from developing the kinds of network they need to thrive at their stage of life. I go on to set out what might be done by way of reform to our framework of public policy to remedy this and to begin to tackle positively network poverty.

The impact of welfare on social networks today

The scope of welfare

The mainstays of our welfare system, including those directly provided by the state and those purchased by way of vouchers, contracts, franchises or grants in aid to private firms and voluntary organisations, are the provision of:

- *money*: income maintenance through the contributory and welfare systems of cash benefits
- *vocational training:* purchased by Training and Enterprise Councils, the European Social Fund and local authority economic development departments
- *social rented housing:* by local authorities, housing associations and other Registered Social Landlords (RSLs), and housing benefit as an earmarked cash benefit to support rent payments and mortgage interest tax relief for owner occupiers
- *counselling, support, rehabilitation and special needs housing services:* for problem users of drugs and alcohol, homeless people, ex-offenders and other clienteles; counselling, temporary refuge and other support for the victims of crime, domestic violence and so on
- *legal support:* financial assistance for those on benefits to use legal services through the Legal Aid scheme, and subsidised access free at the point of use to legal advice through Citizens Advice Bureaux, law centres and advice agencies
- *health care:* through the National Health Service

647

- *child protection, childcare, fostering and adoption:* by local authority social services departments
- *education:* by way of schooling and support for places on college and university courses, with ancillary services such as educational welfare to control truancy, the youth service and provision of leisure services
- *social care:* for the elderly in their own homes, in sheltered accommodation, in residential homes and in nursing homes
- *collective transport* (there is no point in continuing referring to 'public transport' when most bus and rail services are now privately run): subsidised by the taxpayer centrally in the case of rail franchises or locally in the case of some bus lines
- *community development activities:* from the provision of community centres through to the work of field community workers with tenants' groups, youth groups and so forth.

Social networks and welfare for adults

I begin with those services which support adults during that period of their lives when they are normally in the labour market or in active retirement.

Most cash benefits do nothing to encourage or enable people to sustain their networks of weak ties. Almost all are individual entitlements. The incentives to seek work built into the Jobseekers' Allowance and Income Support systems, including the duties to use job clubs, job centres and vocational training, generally encourage unemployed people to focus their effort and attention on the formal labour market institutions, despite the evidence that most people who do make their exits from unemployment and poverty do so through their informal networks and contacts. Moreover, heavy crackdowns on the more minor benefit frauds such as 'working off the cards' may send the wrong signals about the use of informal networks to get work. People can begin the process of getting back into the labour market with such activities and penalising them, while rational from the point of view of the Treasury, may not always make good labour market sense.

There are two encouraging signs, however. One is the present government's commitment that it will relax the 'sixteen hour' rule that made study or volunteering for more than sixteen hours per week incompatible with receipt of benefit. Many people get off benefit through volunteering that gives them contacts and skills they need to get paid work. Both study and volunteering have been shown to stimulate the development of weak ties. The other is the welfare-to-work scheme which should get at least some unemployed people in contact with networks in the labour market where they can form some weak ties that may prove valuable later on. One option within the welfare-to-work scheme will be volunteering in an environmental task force. While volunteering is associated for some with upward mobility, and volunteering alongside other young people of similar inexperience can nevertheless be valuable, the contacts that young people at risk of unemployment most need are not principally of this kind.

Job training in most cases puts unemployed people only in contact with other unemployed people on the same course, who, if they are weakly tied, are links to people who cannot, in most cases, offer them many opportunities for making an exit from poverty and unemployment. Few programmes of job training impart the kinds of skills that people need to work networks of weak ties.

The fact that most job training for unemployed people is done by specialist providers, rather than by being bought in from businesses – where the individuals might, once trained, work – merely compounds the problem. Although some schemes include placements with employers, many do not and not all of the programmes that do are designed to enable trainees to build networks there.

Much social rented housing is highly damaging for the making and maintenance of diverse networks of weak ties. A map of London, for instance, which showed the flows of traffic would leave dark islands where the main large areas of council and housing association estates are. They are deliberately isolated from the rest of the city in a misguided concept of 'community' which has over-emphasised the role of strong ties to neighbours and kin by devoting areas solely to residential use with people much like oneself. When community fails on many such estates, policy makers appear perplexed and dismayed. Yet this result is unsurprising. For the kind of community that poor, unemployed and isolated people need is precisely not the kind of endogamous, strongly tied, inward-looking community that they experience or are able to make on many housing estates. Rather they need the kind of diverse, weakly tied, externally networked, geographically open community that middle class people enjoy. Too many discussions of policy toward socially excluded estates concentrate on 'bootstrapping' or 'capacity building' strategies to build up the local community, at the expense of focusing on external linkages. While recent experiments with mixed tenure seem to be a first step in the right direction,[74] many of them unfortunately remain exercises in simply putting people next door to one another in still isolated single purpose residential areas. They have no reason to know one another and no straightforward way to mix in wider communities of work and leisure.

Only community development initiatives, which represent a tiny fraction of public and private expenditure, effort and priorities, are deliberately and primarily directed at the promotion of networks. Nevertheless, because most community development work is directed at building networks of neighbours and people in similar situations, often within bounded geographical areas of residential housing, it does little to encourage and develop diverse networks of weak ties with little redundancy.

Community development workers often regard the building up of formal organisations in poor communities as a key task. But not all organisations are network friendly. Some only provide individualised services or take up the energy of local informal networks at the expense of other activities that might get people into work more quickly. Other organisations become defensive about their turf to the point that they prove damaging to local networks. In these cases, it might be better for community development workers to concentrate on other activities. More direct micro-level work with informal networks is often not rewarded because the results are less tangible than setting up an organisation and because we have not yet developed effective ways of measuring and auditing the value they add. However, they are often much more effective than some organisation-building strategies.

Many counselling, refuge, rehabilitation and support services for all the clienteles listed above are also individualised. When they bring people together, they usually have similar problems and difficulties. While mutual aid and self-help can indeed be beneficial in overcoming trauma, they do nothing to encourage diverse, weak ties to people unlike oneself, which are the longer-term need.

Most legal support is individually dispensed. Moreover, restriction in class action suits mean that the legal aid system does not even facilitate the cementing of networks of mutual aid among neighbours and other people in similar difficulties.

The NHS's very limited effort in public health preventive work and the wholly individualised conception of health that underlies modern allopathic medicine combine to leave the NHS ill equipped to promote social networks.

More generally, most of the professions involved in providing each of these services tend to see problems as individual affairs, looking for individual solutions. Sometimes that is true. But where there are few or inadequate social networks that even well-equipped and connected people can use, the solutions must start further back.

Supporting collective transport does, as one would expect, assist weak tie networking. However, because most of the poorest areas where unemployed people live are among the worst served by rail, underground or metro and bus services (in London, for example, Hackney has no tube station), the beneficial effect is greatly reduced.

Welfare at the beginning and end of life and strongly tied networks

In an otherwise rather gloomy picture, trends in education offer some comfort about the performance of the welfare state. Recent efforts to increase the involvement of parents in schools seem likely to be beneficial both for children, for whom strong ties are reinforced, and for parents, who may form useful weak ties as they meet one another through involvement with their children's schools. The movement toward greater community involvement and secondary schools' connections with local employers also suggests that educationalists are learning how to better support young adolescents managing the transition between network configurations. The main worry here is that the burgeoning time demands of the National Curriculum may crowd out such developments.

Child protection work has swung sharply away from willingness to place children at risk in the care of the local authority if it can be avoided, and towards fostering and adoption rather than children's homes where it cannot. This makes good network sense. Nevertheless, the continuing and depressingly high levels of young homeless people and young problem drug users who have been in local authority care in children's homes suggests that not only is the system still failing to promote the development of strong ties at the crucial stage, but it is also failing to help them manage the network transition to adult life. The state is still the worst parent anyone can possibly have.

The manner in which discharge of elderly people from hospital geriatric wards is often carried out puts a great deal of stress on their carers and immediate relatives and can often strain their strong ties, thus worsening their long-term prospects.

The shift, since 1993, in social care for the elderly towards domiciliary care and the cutting of budgets for 'non-care' activities such as lunch clubs, specialist transport services and befriending activities has actually worsened the possibility that social care might have any network-enhancing role. While many residential and nursing homes are unappealing places and some are little better than warehousing for the unwanted old, domiciliary care can also be extremely isolating for the already housebound.[75]

To sum up, the performance of the welfare state in supporting the right kinds of social network for the stage in the life course that individuals have reached is not impressive. There are real improvements in education, some small encouraging signs in the design of the benefit system and some compromised efforts in the right direction in child protection, community development and collective transport. But the big spending areas of health care, social care, job training and housing still offer little or nothing to encourage the right kind of networks and do much that does the reverse.

Ways forward for network-friendly reform

Every area of welfare state activity needs to be scrutinised and audited to find ways of improving its impact on the social networks of its intended clientele. More bluntly, there is no point in having a debate about how to finance the welfare state in the twenty first century if we cannot devise a series of systems that do more network good than network harm.

The following principles seem to commend themselves.

- At the very least, the activities of the welfare state should *minimise the incidental harm* they do to the ability and cultural willingness of individuals to sustain the kind of social network they need for their stage of life.
- Where it is feasible, affordable and does not conflict with other overriding goals, the welfare state should attempt to *promote* that ability and willingness in the design of its existing activities or in the course of new programmes that are to be introduced for other reasons. Programmes could sometimes be redesigned to achieve their goals in more network-friendly ways.
- In general, there would have to be good reasons of other kinds for the introduction of new programmes or activities specifically intended to promote networking. The priority for such initiatives would presumably be:
  a) to help the long-term unemployed to make better use of contacts for informal job search methods
  b) to sustain strong ties for children at risk
  c) to sustain appropriate ties for old people at risk of becoming dependent.

Within these general principles, a number of more specific recommendations can perhaps be ventured.

As resources allow, the welfare-to-work scheme could be extended from its present clientele of under-25 year olds. For those on benefit, volunteering could be deemed to be one form of 'actively seeking work'. The aim should be for welfare-to-work to become an institution for social mixing.

The conditions of eligibility for the Jobseeker's Allowance could be reformed to encourage informal methods of job search at least as much as formal ones, if not more.

Training and Enterprise Councils' practice of purchasing specific training for the unemployed from specialist agencies should be abandoned. Not only is much of the training of poor quality, but in most cases it generates almost no real network gains. Where training is to be purchased, it should be purchased from businesses operating in a given field, not from a training provider specialising in unemployed people. There is scope for much wider experimentation with placement and mentoring schemes in which adults who can offer access to valuable contacts take responsibility for guiding young unemployed people through vocational training. For some long-term unemployed people, key skills that the system needs to concentrate on are those involved in cultivating informal weak ties with people who can broker information about work opportunities.

Every effort should be made to break up large, social rented housing estates, to use land-use planning powers to diversify uses in smaller packages of land and to use mixed tenure policies not as a management tool but as a community-building strategy.[76] Adjustments could be made to Standard Spending Assessment formulae to allow and encourage local authorities to subsidise collective transport services to isolated estates.

Priority in approvals for private finance initiative capital investment schemes in new collective transport infrastructure (such as rail and metro lines) should be given to providing access for poor areas currently not served or very badly served.

Community development practice needs to break out of its classical geographical paradigm and its concern with neighbourhood, and recognise that poor people need the kinds of geographically open, diverse, low density networks that middle class people have.[77] It should concentrate less on building formal organisations and more on developing new ways to build networks across and between cities, and making more use of electronic communications systems for this purpose. Programmes of community service and socially and age group mixed summer camps for adolescents may be more important in enabling people to meet and form weak ties with people unlike themselves than traditional neighbourhood based work.

The mutual aid and self-help support bias of the counselling, support, rehabilitation and special needs housing industries should gradually be balanced with more effort at reintegration of individuals with wider networks.

The restrictions in the legal aid scheme on financing for class actions should be removed.

Every effort should be made to phase out the use of children's homes within the next ten years and new alternatives experimented with and developed, including small group homes led by responsible young people and concierges and joint fostering arrangements between two or more families. There may be room to experiment with 'children's foyers' or projects in which responsible young people live with a few others with some support from foster parents who can help them in making their network transitions.

Efforts towards more parental involvement and community and business links in schools should be continued and stepped up. The time demands of the National Curriculum should be controlled to make space for this work. The further education college sector has well-developed programmes in this field, from which the secondary school sector could learn a great deal.

The efforts of the NHS in community health activity, sickness and accident prevention, and health promotion through new kinds of networks should be increased sharply. Procedures for discharge from in-patient stay, particularly for elderly people, should be redesigned to place the minimum strain on strong ties to close relatives and neighbours.

In social care, the rush toward care-based and individualised domiciliary services rather than prevention-centred initiatives should be reversed. We need to prolong the period when old people can make use of both weak and strong ties and design financing systems and care support programmes that minimise strains on strong ties.[78] Both Department of Health guidance and Standard Spending Assessments should reflect the importance of non-care services that sustain social networks.

Beyond rethinking the work of the traditional services of the welfare state, it will be important to design policies in other and new areas that will encourage and enable networking. An obvious first area is that of telephony. Recent research has shown that in some poor areas of Newcastle, only 58 per cent of households subscribe to a telephone service.[79] Some areas of rural poverty have similarly low levels.[80] Government could consider subsidising subscriptions for some of the poorest through some kind of voucher system, as has been tried by local authority social service departments for individual poor elderly persons. Now that access to fax, e-mail and Internet services are increasingly important means of sustaining social networks of every kind, policies to encourage more universal access will be critical to network-friendly policy making.[81]

Sustaining weak links requires time, sometimes outside working hours. As working hours have lengthened since the early 1980s, there has been a growing 'time squeeze' which may be putting a number of weak ties as well as strong ties under strain, especially for low paid workers seeking upward mobility.[82] Labour market regulation to create more opportunities for more flexible working arrangements, of a kind that assist workers rather than only employers, could prove beneficial here.

The finding that most unemployed people get jobs more often through those whom they know rather than through formal labour market institutions has complex and difficult implications for equal opportunities policies. Networks – particularly when are closed, dense or dominated by strong ties – tend to be particularistic,[83] and 'it is hard to distinguish "good" and "bad" particularism, and so difficult to legislate particularism'.[84] It is not that equal opportunities legislation at the point of recruitment is necessarily harmful, but it seems likely that it is certainly not enough simply to extend such formal universalism in order to solve the problems of those currently excluded from social networks sustaining employment. There may be cases of particularism in recruitment that could actually prove beneficial for some socially excluded people.

Conclusion

To make the most of life, we need to bind ourselves with strong ties at the beginning and end of life to a few close relatives and neighbours. In adult life, we also need many diverse loose connections to people as unlike ourselves as possible.

It is, therefore, quite misguided to build policies around the idea of building 'communities' as tightly-knit, bounded societies of people who are as kin to one another, despite the recurrent attractions of this myth from ancient times to modern communitarian thinking.[85]

On the other hand, enabling people to build a wide range of types of social capital is a proper goal for public policy. Achieving it will require radical redesign of the activities of the welfare state.

The fifth giant to be added to Beveridge's famous menagerie is Networklessness. Poverty and long-term unemployment, frailty in old age and suicide and alienation among young people are all problems to which network poverty – or, if you prefer, social exclusion, lack of social capital or lack of the means of trust – is a major contributory factor, and in some cases, perhaps the decisive one. Network poverty can take the form of different problems at different stages of the life course and isolation is a serious risk at any age.

The point of this *Argument* is not to say, like some latter-day Marie Antoinette, 'Let them eat networks!', or to suggest that all that poor people need is a rolodex or an electronic organiser or that everyone ought to lead the lifestyle of a 'yuppie' with a mobile phone and a company lunch expense account. Social networks are not the only thing that poor and unemployed people need: there are many other risk factors at work. But these other risk factors are often refracted by the lens of network poverty, and addressing them without considering how to enable people to sustain the networks they need will not be effective.

The only debate about the future of welfare that is worth having is one about how our system can become part of what sustains the network fabric of our society. If we are serious about ending welfare dependency and social exclusion, then it is pointless to debate the future financing of anything else.

Appendix: Network poverty and culture

In this appendix, I set out in more detail than was possible in Part I a way of understanding the relationship between network poverty and cultures as risk factors in one kind of poverty, namely long-term unemployment.

Since the 1940s,[86] there have been many attempts to understand poverty and to design policies to combat it, in terms of cultures of poor and unemployed people. The early ideas of a single culture of poverty, a heritable culture and a culture that will always reinforce poverty have been abandoned.[87] However, it does not follow that culture is unimportant. Indeed, when the idea of culture is correctly understood among people who think about policy, cultural change may become a key part of how poverty is effectively tackled.

Some more rigorous studies of culture among long-term unemployed people have been done which enable us to begin to explore some of the connections between network structure and culture that policy will have to address.

A major study in the early 1990s of long-term unemployed and poor people in four cities in the Netherlands[88] is one of the few to test empirically on this group any of the leading theories of diversity in cultures – namely, the 'grid-group' theory.[89] This theory argues that cultures will diverge according to two principles: the extent to which they accord priority to the social group or the individual ('group'), and the extent to which they see social life as governed by rules, boundaries and structures and controls ('grid'). Cross-tabulating these dimensions yields a classification of four types of culture, as shown in Figure 4.

Figure 4. Cultural analysis by dimensions of grid and group

Grid ⇧	
Network role: isolate *Stance:* personal withdrawal (eg from others, social order, institutions), eclectic values *View of systems:* capricious *World view:* fatalism (bottom of society) / despotism (top of society)	*Network role:* central community *Stance:* affirmation (eg of social values, social order institutions) by rule-following and strong incorporation of individuals in social order *View of systems:* need structure *World view:* hierarchy
Network role: individualism, markets *Stance:* affirmation (eg of social values, social order institutions) by personal entrepreneurial initiative *View of systems:* robust *World view:* libertarianism	*Network role:* enclave, sect *Stance:* collective withdrawal (eg from perceived 'mainstream'), dissidence *View of systems:* subject to stress, vulnerable *World view:* egalitarianism

⇨ Group

This theory begins from the thesis that because these are the fundamental fractures in culture, only these four types of culture will prove to be stable. Although individuals may, in their social and institutional life, exhibit more than one culture, they will only be able to work with one for any length of time. The risks that individuals perceive as serious will, the theory predicts, systematically reflect their prior culture and their behaviour will be correlated systemically with that culture and risk perception.

The importance of the theory is that offers a link between the configurations of social networks that we might expect to find among different groups of unemployed and poor individuals, and the kind of culture they may exhibit. To be more exact, it can be read as predicting that the following variables will run together: network configuration, ideology or political perception of risks, view of systems, behaviour in the face of risks, and life expectations. For the high grid, low group culture, we would expect something like that shown in Figure 5, which corresponds roughly to at least one of the conventional views of the dependency culture or else to one part of a composite conventional view.[90]

Figure 5. Cultural theory predictions for high grid, low group culture

Variable	Value
network configuration	isolated
ideology or political perception of risks	fatalism
view of systems, eg labour market, welfare state	capricious, arbitrary
behaviour in the face of risks	retreat, discouragement, acceptance of dependency
life expectations	pessimistic

The Dutch study of unemployed people found that the theory appeared to have some force, but that things were a little more complicated than this simple prediction. These researchers found the following cultural groups among the long-term unemployed:

- very few, if any, true hierarchists (although other researchers would have classified as hierarchists some of the people they put into other categories)
- two kinds of individualists, which they classified as the *calculating* (9 per cent who 'worked' the benefits system and did not seek a job) and the *enterprising* (10 per cent who sought work and income in the informal economy but also sought work in the formal labour market)
- two kinds of enclavists, which they classified as the *conformists* (the largest group at 36 per cent who strove for paid employment, sought training and complied with benefit rules: other scholars might have regarded them as hierarchists) and the *ritualists* (9 per cent who went through the motions of job search and compliance with social norms, albeit without real hope: other scholars would perhaps have split this group between hierarchists and isolates)
- a group whom they call *autonomous* (10 per cent who rejected the goals of work and social respectability and focused on volunteering, study or hobbies, made little use of the informal economy but made ends meet on their legal entitlement to welfare; other scholars would probably have regarded this group as a type of enclavists)
- a relatively small number of isolates whom they called *retreatists* (25 per cent who had become discouraged, resigned to exclusion

from the labour market, but who made no effort to work in the informal economy or cheat the benefit system); the study also found that the longer a person is out of work, the more likely they are to become a retreatist, particularly if they began as a conformist.[91]

The study also collected data on social links and social 'bonding', reporting – consistently with the theory's prediction of high group, low grid cultures – that conformists and ritualists exhibited the greatest 'neighbourhood bonding' but within narrow closed groups.[92] Enterprising individualists had extensive, open networks – presumably, although the authors do not put it in these terms, with a reasonable number of weak hole-spanning links. Fatalistic retreatists were indeed isolated, with only 18 per cent of them maintaining links with friends who lived elsewhere in their city, and only 29 per cent of them with a large network of friends. The autonomous, living mainly in big cities, networked mainly in their own bohemian quarters, and maintained narrow, interest-focused networks, as one would expect from enclavists.[93] Broadly, the findings of this study suggest that one can find examples of people for whom the five types of variable take the predicted values, linking network configuration and culture as expected. But – whether due to problems with classifying individuals or because of real differences, it is hard to tell – there are perhaps at least some isolates whose networks may not be quite so confined and the congruence between the predicted values may be less neat than the theory suggests.

Cultural theorists do not, unfortunately, speak with one voice on the question of the direction of line of causation between culture and network configuration. The anthropological reading, which stresses the isolate and enclave aspects of the two alienated cultures, sometimes tends to suggest that network features drive culture.[94] By contrast, the 'California' reading of the theory, which stresses fatalism and egalitarianism as ideological risk perceptions, sometimes tends to suggest that culture drives network configuration,[95] although there are passages in the texts of both schools that can be read in the other way. Presumably, as I argued in the simplified model of risk factors for unemployment set out in Figure 2, network and culture influence one another as a part of a general social system, but the balance of influence in any particular case still needs to be understood better. At any rate, the attempt to reduce the one to the other, in order to enable policy makers to tackle only one of them, is probably misguided.

However, the central finding of the Dutch study is that those with open, extensive networks and with an enterprising, calculating or at least autonomous culture, thrived much better than those who were isolated or who had narrow networks and retreatist or ritualist cultures.[96] The combination of the right network configuration and the right culture, whatever the causal links between the two, is centrally important.

This suggests a number of ways forward for public policy, which are explored in Part I of this *Argument*. Certainly, it is clear that interventions that can enable people to sustain their networks are likely to have some value in preventing them slipping in retreatism. Strategies that identify ritualists at an early stage of unemployment and find ways to connect them with others – through weak ties – who may be of use to them may be particularly valuable.

Acknowledgements

In writing this *Argument*, I have drawn shamelessly on my networks of both strong and weak ties for a wide variety of intellectual resources. In particular, I am grateful to the following people for their comments on an earlier draft. None of them bears any responsibility for my opinions, policy recommendations, errors or misunderstandings: Helmut Anheier, Tom Bentley, John Browning, Ian Christie, Mary Douglas, Howard Gardner, Ben Jupp, Diana Leat, Carl Milofsky, Lydia Morris, Geoff Mulgan, Ray Pahl, Helen Perry, Jo Anne Schneider, Marilyn Taylor, Peter Taylor-Gooby, Claire Wenger and Helen Wilkinson: many of them were present at a Demos seminar on 3 July 1997 at which these ideas were presented.

Notes

[1] Hall, 1997, 14. He cites the following sources for these findings, Oakley and Rajan, 1991; Bulmer, 1986; Goldthorpe, 1987, ch. 7; Allan, 1990; Stacey *et al*, 1975; Goldthorpe *et al*, 1968.

[2] Tyrrell, 1995, 23.

[3] Willmott, 1987, cited in Pahl and Spencer, 1997, 3.

[4] Pahl and Spencer, 1997.

[5] For an account of the continuing importance of such networks of informal exchange among longstanding local working class residents in an area of declining economic importance of traditional industries and in-migration of more cosmopolitan urban working class people, see Milofsky, 1997a.

[6] Granovetter, 1973.

[7] Grieco, 1987.

[8] Granovetter, 1973,1361.

[9] Lin and Vaughn, 1981; Lin, 1982, 1988; Flap and de Graaf, 1986, all cited in Coleman, 1990, 302.

[10] Daniel, 1990, 76ff.

[11] As reported in Morris, 1995, 27-28.

[12] Schneider, 1997a.

[13] Personal communication from Helmut Anheier.

[14] Burt, 1992.

[15] Burt, 1997, for a general review of the significance of this finding for personal attainment and failure, see Breiger, 1995. Merton argued that success and honour for scientists was in some large part a function of their social networks. To be trained by one who had achieved glittering prizes and to write with such a luminary, and to have the great professor give one introductions and contacts, gave the young scientist an advantage over those with similar intellectual endowment but fewer social network resources. Moreover, the weak tie effect was strengthened, Merton argued, by the fact that, at least to some extent, great scientists prefer splendid isolation; rather than to be surrounded by potential successors and rivals, they prefer to send their star pupils out to other universities after nurturing them: Merton,1988.

[16] Dean and Taylor-Gooby, 1992, 112-3.

[17] Daniel, 1990, 93-4.

[18] Paugam, 1995, 62-3.

[19] Gallie *et al*, 1994, 255.

[20] Gallie *et al*, 1994, 256, table 8:15.

[21] Gallie *et al*, 1994, 252.

[22] Gallie *et al*, 1994, 255.

[23] Pahl, 1997.

[24] Morris, 1995, ch. 2.

[25] Morris, 1995, ch. 2.

[26] Morris, 1995, 33. I am grateful to Ben Jupp for pointing out that the Manchester School in anthropology found in the 1960s, in a series of studies of social ties among

people moving from the countryside to the cities in Zambia, that in conditions of high unemployment and high levels of competition for jobs, strong ties reassert themselves as the key means of securing work; for the same reasons as those suggested by Morris for working class people in Hartlepool in its period of economic decline, see Mitchell, 1969.

[27] Wilson, 1987, 1991, 1996.

[28] Wilson, 1996, 65.

[29] Wilson, 1996, 76.

[30] Schneider, 1997.

[31] Wilson, 1965.

[32] Fukuyama, 1995.

[33] Schneider, 1997b.

[34] Zucker, 1986; 6, 1994.

[35] Milofsky, 1997a.

[36] In formal terms, the network position of these individuals exhibits high betweenness and centrality, see Scott, 1991, ch. 5. A simple case is that of *tertius gaudens* or the third person who, operating between two others, is able to play them off against each other, benefit from their conflict by arbitrating, or making each beholden to her or him. The *tertius* can reap and hold information benefits, but those who become beholden may still be better off than they would if they did not encounter the *tertius* at all, Burt, 1992, 30ff.

[37] Or, as Gallie *et al* (1994,252) put it, an 'unmeasured background variable'.

[38] Goldthorpe, 1987; cited in Hall 1997, 16.

[39] Gallie *et al*, 1994.

[40] Daniel, 1990.

[41] Daniel, 1990; Gallie *et al*, 1994; Payne *et al*, 1996; Smith, 1992; Mingione, 1996.

[42] Emler and Reicher, 1995, 57, 123, 156, 174-7.

[43] Gambetta, 1988, see also the discussion in Putnam, 1993, 145-148, and in Fukuyama, 1995, 101, all three have drawn on Banfield's 1958 study of 'amoral familism' in the Italian south.

[44] Milofsky, 1997b.

[45] The main body of psychological work on this point is attachment theory. For a review of the main findings of this tradition of research on the importance of strong ties to kin for child health, see Wilkinson *et al*, 1997, 199-203 and Sainsbury 1997, 204-218 in the same volume. For a general review, see Fonagy, 1996.

[46] Moore *et al*, 1995; Hutson and Liddiard, 1994; Jencks, 1994; Boulton, 1993, 136-8.

[47] Boulton, 1993, 138.

[48] Moore *et al*, 1995, 181ff.

[49] Moore *et al*, 1995, 130.

[50] Mitchell, 1975, 48-51.

[51] Wilkinson, 1996, 164.

[52] Brunner, 1996, 290.

[53] Source of figure, Wenger 1997.

[54] Hendry *et al*, 1993, ch. 6 and 7.

[55] The skills may correspond roughly to the ability to deploy what in social psychology are known – following Bernstein 1961 – as more elaborated codes, by contrast with restricted codes; I am grateful to Howard Gardner for this suggestion.

[56] Room, 1995 provides a good recent review of multi-dimensional measures. Townsend, 1979, as summarised by Whelan and Whelan, 1995, included 'social relations' as the last of twelve dimensions in his taxonomy. Muffels, 1993, also reported in Whelan and Whelan, 1995, lists social participation and social contacts as elements of his Social Deprivation Scale.

[57] Tosi, 1996; Silver, 1996.

[58] Berghman, 1995, reports an Irish study which argued that one element of a four part definition of social exclusion was defined as 'interpersonal integration' into 'the family and community system'. The others were concerned with democratic and legal rights, labour market and welfare state entitlements. However, that study seems to make no particular case about the typical direction of the lines of causation between the four dimensions of social exclusion. By contrast, in this *Argument*, I want to suggest a specific place in a causal system, whereby network poverty is not necessarily the major cause of entry into long-term unemployment, but one of the key causes of failure to exit from it.

[59] Burt, 1997; Douglas has recently gone further and identified having the right kind of social network not only with social capital, but with what Bourdieu, 1991, would call symbolic capital, or, in her terms, the competent command of the stock of names, Douglas, 1997.

[60] Bourdieu, 1991. For detailed discussion of the definition of social capital, its origins and types, see the archived e-mail discussion, 'Social capital' from the SOCNET listserve, available on the World Wide Web site of the International Society for Social Network Analysis: http://www.heinz.cmu.edu/project/INSNA/ arc_soc/capital.html

[61] Coleman, 1990, ch. 12, Putnam 1993; Hall, 1997. Coleman's characterisation of social capital is slippery, but he talks of it as the set of resources that are afforded by the social relations in which an individual is involved. This suggests that he regards social capital as accumulated with the simple accumulation of more ties of any kind. He also talks of the important social relations as those that are characterised by trust and obligation. Weak ties, typically do not demand or offer a great deal of trust and mutual obligation by contrast with strong ties to kin. When Coleman speaks of closed and dense (highly redundant) social networks as ones with high social capital, he seems to be talking about ones with rather strong ties. By linking social capital with norms, obligations and favours, rather than with network opportunities in general, his conception is unduly narrow. To the extent that his argument suggests that an individual would maximise strong ties in order to maximise social capital, then it seems misleading. The argument that I make out here suggests that Coleman's conception of social capital is not adequate to capture the specific network features that make for social capital. However, one of Coleman's valuable insights – though one hard to reconcile with his general account – is that much social capital is a by-product of other transactions, and that ties developed for one purpose are 'appropriated' for other uses. This describes well the uses to which many middle class people put their weak ties.

[62] Putnam, 1995, 664-5.

[63] In cultural theoretic terms, this is the most enclavist level.

[64] 6, 1994.

[65] Coleman, 1990, talks of information itself as a form of social capital: I prefer to stress the practice of making it available as the social aspect; Bourdieu and Wacquant, 1992, 119 also stress this level of social capital in their definition.

[66] This is the level of social capital on which Putnam, 1993, places the greatest stress: 1993, 169.

[67] Coleman, 1990, speaks of norms as a 'form' of social capital (eg 310), and develops models for the ways in which they can emerge from activity and transactions across networks.

[68] This is what I want to take from Fukuyama's 1995 concept of 'spontaneous sociability' as a 'subset' of social capital: 1995, 27. However, his characterisation seems to run together ability to organise (on which I focus) with willingness (which is more a more complex matter) with the product or organisation itself. The idea of 'spontaneity', with its air of being without clear social cause, is one that social capital theory, can do without.

[69] Despite the suggestions of Putnam, 1993, to this effect: for the full argument here, see 6 and Leat, 1997.

[70] 6, 1994.

[71] Granovetter, 1985.

[72] White, 1981.

[73] Castells, 1996.

[74] See Page D and Boughton B, 1997, for one study of four mixed tenure experiments that suggests – although it is too early to make a definitive evaluation, and the study is largely description and based on a very small sample of opportunity – that there is a case that there may be slow incremental gains in social network configurations.

[75] Leat and 6, 1997.

[76] In a recent review of the policy implications of social networks at a community level in the US, Sampson (1997, 41) argues essentially the same case for dispersal of concentrations of public housing.

[77] For all their faults, this was one of the aims of the turn-of-the-century settlements such as Toynbee Hall in the East End of London or Hull House in Chicago, which brought middle class people into working class areas to make specific individual contacts.

[78] 6 and Leat, 1997.

[79] Graham, 1997.

[80] Gillespie and Cornford, 1996.

[81] IBM and CDF, 1997.

[82] Demos, 1994.

[83] Taylor and Hoggett, 1994.

[84] Heimer, 1992, 145.

[85] For a history of the idea, see Black, 1984; for a contemporary critique of communitarian thinking on this ground, see Pahl, 1997, and Pahl and Spencer, 1997. It is a moot point how far Etzioni, the leading communitarian thinker, can be impugned

on this charge. While some of his rhetoric about ties that 'bind' and stress on the family does suggest that he values principally strong ties, his talk of 'balance', pluralism and his occasional recognition of the distinctive social structure of cities may be sufficient to exonerate him from some of Pahl's strictures. But certainly, the general tenor of his work is to be suggest in the reader a suspicion of a life dominated by weak ties as anomic, irresponsible and excessively individualist; see Etzioni, 1993.

[86] Lewis, 1968.

[87] The comprehensive array of critiques brought together by Townsend, 1979, 65-71, not only convinced many people that the ideas of a vicious cycle of poverty and the sub-culture of poverty offered by Lewis and others were misconceived, but that the idea of culture had no place in discussions of poverty. In the 1980s and early 1990s in the USA, some of the writings of Charles Murray resurrected the argument that the poor are locked into a culture that reinforces their poverty, although Murray also sometimes seemed to argue that culture was irrelevant and only financial incentives mattered in explaining how poor people persist in or exit from poverty and unemployment, Murray, 1984; 1990. Wilson 1996, 66ff also handles the theme of cultural transmission over local networks by role models and parenting in ghettos, but generally avoids the determinism or the assertion of a single culture, and the assertion of individual fecklessness that characterises some of the writings of neo-conservatives from the late Lord Joseph to Charles Murray on this theme.

[88] Engberson et al, 1993.

[89] Developed by anthropologist Mary Douglas, political scientist Aaron Wildavsky, geographer Michael Thompson and their students, see Douglas 1970, 1985, 1986, 1992a, 1992b, 1996; Douglas and Wildavsky, 1982; Douglas and Isherwood, 1979; Thompson, Ellis and Wildavsky, 1990; Coyle and Ellis, 1994; Rayner, 1992; Dake and Wildavsky, 1992; Adams, 1995; 6, 1997.

[90] cf. Dean and Taylor-Gooby, 1992.

[91] Engberson et al 1993, seem to have mapped the grid-group classification of cultures onto the classification of 'modes of individual adaptation' to 'institutional norms' or 'culture patterns' proposed by Merton, 1938, 139, as part of a theory of deviance.

[92] Engberson et al, 162ff.

[93] Consistently with cultural theory, Castells, 1997, argues that such enclave networks, of which urban social movements are typical, tend to be defensive and reactive.

[94] Douglas, 1970, 1996.

[95] Thompson et al, 1990.

[96] Engberson et al, ch. 9.

References

Adams J, 1995, *Risk*, UCL Press, London.

Allan G, 1990, 'Class variation in friendship patterns' in *British Journal of Sociology*, 389-392.

Banfield EC, 1958, *The moral basis of a backward society*, Free Press, Glencoe, Illinois.

Berghman J, 1995, 'Social exclusion in Europe: policy context and analytical framework' in Room G, ed, 1995, *Beyond the threshold: the measurement and analysis of social exclusion*, Policy Press, Bristol, 10-28.

Bernstein B, 1961, 'Social class and linguistic development: a theory of social learning', in Halsey AH, Floud J, and Anderson CA, 1961, *Education, economy and society*, Free Press, New York.

Black A, 1984, *Guilds and civil society in European thought from the twelfth century to the present*, Methuen, London.

Boulton I, 1993, 'Youth homelessness and health care' in Fisher K and Collins J, eds, 1993, *Homelessness, health care and welfare provision*, Routledge, London, 136-148.

Bourdieu P, 1991, *Language and symbolic power*, Polity Press, Cambridge.

Bourdieu P and Wacquant L, 1992, *An invitation to reflexive sociology*, University of Chicago Press, Chicago.

Breiger RL, 195, 'Social structure and the phenomenology of attainment', *American Review of Sociology*, no 21, 115-136.

Brunner E, 1996, 'The social and biological basis of cardiovascular disease in office workers' in Blane D, Brunner E and Wilkinson R, eds,1996, *Health and social organisation: towards a health policy for the 21st century*, Routledge, London, 272-299.

Bulmer M, 1986, *Neighbours: the work of Philip Abrams*, Cambridge University Press, Cambridge.

Burt RS, 1992, *Structural holes: the social structure of competition*, University of Chicago Press, Chicago.

Burt RS, 1997 forthcoming, 'The contingent structure of social capital' in *Administrative Science Quarterly*.

Castells M, 1996, *The information age: economy, society and culture, Volume I – The rise of the network society*, Blackwell, Oxford.

Castells M, 1996, *The information age: economy, society and culture, Volume II – The power of identity*, Blackwell, Oxford.

Coleman, JS, 1990, *Foundations of social theory*, Harvard University Press, Cambridge, Massachusetts.

Coyle DJ and Ellis RJ, 1994, *Politics, policy and culture*, Westview Press, Boulder, Colorado.

Dake K, and Wildavsky A, 1992; 'Theories of risk perception: who fears what and why?' in Burger E Jr, ed. 1992, *Risk*, University of Michigan Press, Ann Arbor, Michigan.

Daniel WW, 1990, *The unemployed flow*, Policy Studies Institute, London.

Dean H and Taylor-Gooby P, 1992, *Dependency culture: the explosion of a myth*, Harvester Wheatsheaf, Hemel Hempstead.

The time squeeze, Demos Quarterly, issue 5.

Douglas 1970, *Natural symbols: explorations in cosmology*, 1996 edn, Routledge, London.

Douglas M and Isherwood B, 1979, *The world of goods: toward an anthropology of consumption*, 1996 edn, Routledge, London.

Douglas M and Wildavsky A, 1982, *Risk and culture: an essay on the selection of technological and environmental dangers*, University of California Press, Berkeley, California.

Douglas M, 1986, *How institutions think*, Routledge and Kegan Paul, London.

Douglas M, 1992a, *Risk and blame: essays in cultural theory*, Routledge, London.

Douglas M, 1992b, 'Risk as a forensic resource' in Burger E Jr, ed, 1992, *Risk*, University of Michigan Press, Ann Arbor, Michigan.

Douglas M, 1996; *Thought styles*, Sage, London.

Douglas M, 1997, 'Poverty as caused by exclusion', paper given at a conference at Padua University, 21 May 1997.

Douglas M,1985, *Risk acceptability according to the social sciences*, Russell Sage Foundation, New York.

Emler N and Reicher S, 1995, *Adolescence and delinquency: the collective management of reputation*, Blackwell, Oxford.

Engberson G, Schuyt K, Timmer J, van Waarden F, 1993, *Cultures of unemployment: a comparative look at long-term unemployment and urban poverty*, Westview Press, Boulder, Colorado.

Etzioni, A, 1993, *The spirit of community: rights, responsibilities and the communitarian agenda*, 2nd edn, HarperCollins, London.

Flap HD and de Graaf ND, 1986, 'Social capital and attained occupational status' in *Netherlands Journal of Sociology* 22, 145-161.

Fonagy P, 1996, 'Patterns of attachment, interpersonal relationships and health' in Blane D, Brunner E and Wilkinson R, eds, 1996, *Health and social organisation: towards a health policy for the 21st century*, Routledge, London.

Fukuyama F, 1995, *Trust: the social virtues and the source of prosperity*, Hamish Hamilton, London.

Gambetta D, 1988, 'Mafia: the price of distrust', in Gambetta D, ed, 1988, *Trust: making and breaking co-operative relations*, Cambridge University Press, Cambridge.

Gallie D, Marsh C and Vogler C, eds, 1994, *Social change and the experience of unemployment*, Oxford University Press, Oxford.

Gillespie A and Cornford J, 1996, 'Telecommunication infrastructures and regional development' in Dutton WH, ed, 1996, *Information and communication technologies: visions and realities*, Oxford University Press, Oxford.

Goldthorpe JH, 1987, *Social mobility and class structure in modern Britain*, 2nd edn, Clarendon Press, Oxford.

Goldthorpe JH, Lockwood D, Bechhofer F and Platt J, 1968, *The affluent worker: political attitudes and behaviour*, Cambridge University Press, Cambridge.

Graham SDN, 1997, 'Access to the telephone and information exclusion', presentation to the Demos seminar, *Virtually social: information exclusion*, IBM, London, 6 May 1997.

Granovetter MS, 1973, 'The strength of weak ties' in *American Journal of Sociology*, no 78, 1360-1380.

Granovetter MS, 1985, 'Economic action and social structure: the problem of embeddedness', *American journal of sociology*, 91, 481-510, reprinted in Granovetter MS and Swedberg R, eds, 1992, *The sociology of economic life*, Westview Press, Boulder, Colorado, 53-81.

Grieco M, 1987, *Keeping it in the family*, Tavistock, London.

Hall, PA, 1997, *Social capital in Britain*, Centre for European Studies, Harvard University, Cambridge, Massachusetts.

Heimer CA, 1992, 'Doing your job *and* helping your friends: universalistic norms about obligations to particular others in networks' in Nohria N and Eccles RG, eds, 1992, *Networks and organisations: structure, form and action*, Harvard Business School Press, Cambridge, Massachusetts.

Hendry LB, Shucksmith J, Love JG and Glendinning A, 1993, *Young people's leisure and lifestyles*, Routledge, London.

Hutson S and Liddiard M, 1994, *Youth homelessness: the construction of a social issue*, MacMillan, Basingstoke.

IBM and Community Development Foundation, 1997, *The net result: social inclusion in the information society*, IBM and CDF, London.

Jencks C, 1994, *The homeless*, Harvard University Press, Cambridge, Massachusetts.

Leat D and 6 P, 1997, *Holding back the years: how Britain can grow old better in the twenty first century*, Demos, London.

Lewis O, 1968, 'The culture of poverty' in Moynihan DP, ed, 1968, *On understanding poverty*, Basic Books, New York.

Lin N, 1982, 'Social resources and instrumental action' in Marsden P and Lin N, eds, 1982, *Social structure and network analysis*, Sage, Beverly Hills, California,131-145.

Lin N, 1988,'Social resources and social mobility: a structural theory of status attainment' in Breiger RL, ed, 1988, *Social mobility and social structure*, Cambridge University Press, Cambridge.

Lin M, Ensel WM, and Vaughn JC, 1981, 'Social resources and the strength of ties', structural factors in occupational status attainment' in *American Sociological Review*, no 46, 393-405.

Merton RK, 1938, 'Social structure and anomie', *American Sociological Review*, no 3, 672-682, reprinted in excerpted form in Merton RK, 1996, *On social structure and social science*, ed. by Sztompka P, University of Chicago Press, Chicago, 132-152.

Merton RK, 1988, 'The Matthew effect in science II: cumulative advantage and the symbolism of intellectual property' in *Isis*, no 79, 607-623, reprinted in excerpted form in Merton RK, 1996, *On social structure and social science*, ed. by Sztompka P, University of Chicago Press, Chicago, 318-336.

Milofsky C, 1997a, 'Two cultures of work in central Pennsylvania: institutional supports for working class values', paper given at the conference, *Postmodern culture, global capitalism and democratic action*, College Park, University of Maryland, 10-13 April 1997.

Milofsky, C, 1997b, personal communication.

Mingione E, ed, 1996, *Urban poverty and the underclass: a reader*, Blackwell, Oxford.

Mitchell JC, ed, 1969, *Social networks in urban situations: analyses of personal relationships in central African towns*, Manchester University Press, Manchester.

Mitchell R, 1975, *Depression*, Penguin, Harmondsworth.

Moore J, Canter D, Stockley D and Drake M, 1995, *The faces of homelessness in London*, Dartmouth, Aldershot.

Morris LD, 1995, *Social divisions: economic decline and social structural change*, UCL Press, London.

Muffels R, 1993, *Welfare effects of social security: essays on poverty, social security and the labour market*, Report 21, Social Security Series, KUB, Tilburg.

Murray C, 1984, *Losing ground: American social policy 1950-1980*, Basic Books, New York.

Murray C, 1990, *The emerging British underclass*, Choice in Welfare Series No. 2, Health and Welfare Unit, Institute for Economic Affairs, London.

Oakley A and Rajan L, 1991, 'Social class and social support: the same or different?' in *Sociology*, vol 25, no 1, 31-59.

Page D and Boughton B, 1997, *Mixed tenure housing estates*, Notting Hill Home Ownership, London.

Pahl RE, 1997, 'The ties that bind: creating communities', paper presented at the ESRC conference, *Future Britain: revitalising policy through research*, 25 June 1997, London.

Pahl, RE and Spencer L, 1997 forthcoming, 'The politics of friendship', *Renewal*, autumn.

Paugam S, 1995, 'The spiral of precariousness: a multidimensional approach to the process of social disqualification in France' in Room G, ed, 1995, *Beyond the threshold: the measurement and analysis of social exclusion*, Policy Press, Bristol, 49-79.

Payne J, Casey B, Payne C, and Connolly S, 1996, *Long-term unemployment: individual risk factors and outcomes*, Policy Studies Institute, London.

Putnam RD with Leonard R and Nanetti RY, 1993, *Making democracy work: civic traditions in modern Italy*, University of Princeton Press, Princeton, New Jersey.

Putnam RD, 1995, 'Tuning in, tuning out: the strange disappearance of social capital in America', *Political science and politics*, December, 664-683.

Rayner S, 1992, 'Cultural theory and risk analysis' in Krimsky S and Golding D, eds, 1992, *Social theories of risk*, Praeger, Westport, Connecticut.

Room G, ed, 1995, *Beyond the threshold: the measurement and analysis of social exclusion*, Policy Press, Bristol.

Sainsbury J, 1997, 'The benefits to children of paid parental leave' in Wilkinson H, with Radley R, Christie I, Lawson G and Sainsbury J, 1997, *Time out: the costs and benefits of paid parental leave*, Demos, London, 204-218.

Sampson RJ, 1997, *What community supplies*, Brookings Institution, Washington DC.

Schneider JA, 1997a, 'Pathways to opportunity: the role of race, social networks, institutions and neighbourhood in career and educational paths for people on welfare', paper presented at the 27th annual Urban Affairs Association meeting, 27 April 1997, Toronto.

Schneider JA, 1997b, personal communication.

Scott, J, 1991, *Social network analysis: a handbook*, Sage, London.

Silver H, 1996, 'Culture, politics and national discourses of the new urban poverty', in Mingione E, ed, 1996, *Urban poverty and the underclass: a reader*, Blackwell, Oxford.

Smith DJ, ed, 1992, *Understanding the underclass*, Policy Studies Institute, London.

Stacey M, Batstone E, Bell C and Murcott A, 1975, *Power, persistence and change*, Routledge and Kegan Paul, London.

Taylor M and Hoggett P, 1994, 'Trusting in networks? The third sector and welfare change?' in 6 P and Vidal I, eds, 1994, *Delivering welfare: repositioning non-profit and co-operative action in western European welfare states*, CIES, Barcelona, 125-149.

Thompson M, Ellis R and Wildavsky A, 1990, *Cultural theory*, Westview Press, Boulder, Colorado.

Tosi A, 1996, 'The excluded and the homeless: the social construction of the fight against poverty in Europe' in Mingione E, ed, 1996, *Urban poverty and the underclass: a reader*, Blackwell, Oxford.

Townsend P, 1979, *Poverty in the United Kingdom*, Penguin, Harmondsworth.

Tyrrell B, 1995, 'Time in our lives: facts and analysis on the 90s' in *The time squeeze, Demos Quarterly*, issue 5, 23-25.

Wenger C, 1997, 'Social networks and the prediction of elderly people at risk', paper given at the Royal College of Psychiatrists conference, *Psychiatry of old age*, Windermere, 10-12 April 1997.

Whelan BJ and Whelan CT, 1995, 'In what sense is poverty multi-dimensional?' in Room G, ed, 1995, *Beyond the threshold: the measurement and analysis of social exclusion*, Policy Press, Bristol, 29-48.

White HC, 1981, 'Varieties of markets' in Wellman N and Berkowitz SD, eds, 1988, *Social structures: a network approach*, Cambridge University Press, Cambridge, 226-260.

Wilkinson H, with Radley R, Christie I, Lawson G and Sainsbury J, 1997, *Time out: the costs and benefits of paid parental leave*, Demos, London.

Wilkinson R, 1996, *Unhealthy societies: the afflictions of inequality*, Routledge, London.

Willmott P, 1987, *Friendship networks and social support: a study in a London suburb*, Policy Studies Institute, London.

Wilson WJ, 1987, *The truly disadvantaged: the inner city, the underclass and public policy*, University of Chicago Press, Chicago.

Wilson, WJ, 1991, 'Studying inner city dislocations' in *American Sociological Review*, no 56, 1-14.

Wilson WJ, 1996, *When work disappears: the new world of the urban poor*, Alfred A Knopf, New York.

Winkfield N, 1995, 'Bad timing: attitudes to the new world of work' in *The time squeeze, Demos Quarterly*, issue 5, 26-29.

Zucker LG, 1986, 'The production of trust: institutional sources of economic structure, 1840-1920' in Bacharach S, eds, 1986, *Research in organisational behaviour*, JAI Press, Greenwich, Connecticut, 8, 53-111.

6 P, 1994, *Trust, social theory and public policy*, Demos, London and School of Social Science, University of Bath, Bath.

6 P, 1997, 'Housing policy in the risk archipelago: toward holistic and anticipatory government', keynote paper given to the Housing Studies Association annual conference, 2 April 1997, University of York, forthcoming in *Housing studies*.

6 P and Leat D, 1997, 'Inventing the British voluntary sector by committee: from Wolfenden to Deakin' in *Non-Profit Studies*, vol 1, no 2, 33-46.